How to Receive God's Power with Gifts of the Spirit

~

How to Operate in the Gifts

~

By Prince Handley

University of Excellence Press
Handley WORLD SERVICES Publishing
P.O. Box A
Downey, California 90241 USA

TABLE OF CONTENTS

FOREWARD

Many who refute the Gifts of the Holy Spirit as being valid for **today** readily agree that they were necessary for the Early Jewish Believers. The Gifts of the Holy Spirit have not ceased (including tongues). If God's People ever needed assistance by the Spirit it is **now**. Impending crises are enveloping the world, and many "signs" show that we are in transition to the Last Days.

The Baptism in the Holy Spirit is NOT the same as the Baptism into the Body of Messiah. All Jesus' followers have the Holy Spirit; However, **NOT all of His followers have the Baptism in the Holy Spirit**. This gift of power is PROMISED to **you**, the believer. It is the Promise from on high!

I have revised this book to make it easier to understand **how to receive** the Baptism in the Holy Spirit. Plus, you will learn: 1. **What are the Gifts** of the Spirit; and, 2. **How to operate** in the Gifts of the Spirit.

There are many attributes of ... and advantages to ... the Gifts of the Holy Spirit operating in your life in areas such as relationships, ministry, business, and personal. You will learn these in this book.

As you prayerfully read this book, you can experience NEW power and productivity for the End Times.

How TO RECEIVE GOD'S POWER WITH GIFTS OF THE SPIRIT

The wonderful thing about knowing Jesus is that life gets fuller every day - if you let it! When Christ died on the cross for your sins, his blood paid for your sins AND bought your freedom. Jesus wants you to tell others about this "Good News": how to be free, forgiven of sins, and filled with God's POWER.

The God of Israel is the only God. He is a "God of Power" who loves you. He raised his son, Jesus, from the dead. Shortly before Jesus went back to Heaven, he said that IN HIS NAME " ... the message about repentance and the forgiveness of sins must be preached to all nations ..." [Luke 24:47]

Jesus didn't ask you to do this job alone. He promised to send you a "gift" of POWER which would help you. Jesus said that he would send this promise upon you himself. "And I, myself, will send upon you what my Father has promised." [Luke 24:49]

The book of Acts in the New Testament of the Holy Bible tells you how to receive this "gift" (the promise of the Father). The Holy Spirit used a man named Luke, who was a follower of Jesus, to write both the book of Acts and the book of Luke. In the book of Luke, Luke tells us how Jesus did his miracles by the POWER of the Holy Spirit. In the book of Acts, Luke tells us how the early followers of Jesus did their miracles by the POWER of the Holy Spirit.

You, also - as a follower of Jesus - are to do the same miracles by the POWER of the Holy Spirit! As a matter of fact, Jesus said, "Whoever believes in me will do the works I do - yes, he will do even greater ones, for I am going to the Father." [John 14:12]

Jesus was taken up into Heaven, he told his followers that God, the Father, had promised them a "gift". "But wait for the promise of the Father ... for John truly baptized with water; but you shall be BAPTIZED WITH THE HOLY SPIRIT not many days from now." [Acts 1:4-5]

The promise of the Father, the "gift" which Jesus said he would send upon his followers when he went back to Heaven, was made to you, also! "For God's promise was made to you and your children, and TO ALL who are far away - ALL whom the Lord our God calls to himself." [Acts 2:39]

6

The Holy Spirit lives in all those who follow Jesus; but to be "baptized" with the Holy Spirit is an extra gift. In John 20:22, after Christ died on the cross and rose up from the grave (before he went back to Heaven), Jesus breathed on his followers and said, "Receive the Holy Spirit."

After this, the Holy Spirit was IN THEM, but as yet they had NOT been "baptized" with the Holy Spirit. Jesus is our "Baptizer", just as he is our Savior, our Healer, and our Deliverer. In all four Gospels plus the book of Acts we find: "John baptized with water ... but Jesus baptizes with the Holy Spirit." [Matthew 3:11; Mark 1:8; Luke 3:16; John 1:33; and Acts 1:4-5]

To be "baptized" means to be overwhelmed or covered with, This is why Jesus told his followers (even though the Holy Spirit was already IN THEM), " ... wait in the city until the POWER from above comes down upon you." [Luke 24:49]

Jesus said his followers would be filled with POWER when the Holy Spirit came on them. He said they would be witnesses for him. "But you shall receive power, after the Holy Spirit has come upon you: and you shall be witnesses for me ... to the ends of the earth." [Acts 1:8]

ℕ ℕ ℕ

In Acts Chapter Two (verses 1-4) we read what happened as the followers of Jesus waited in the city of Jerusalem. As a result of their being "filled" with the Spirit they began to SPEAK WITH OTHER TONGUES.

"And when the day of Pentecost had arrived, they [the believers] were all with one accord in one place. And suddenly there came a sound from Heaven like a rushing mighty wind, and it filled all the house where they were sitting. And there appeared unto them tongues like fire that separated and sat on each of them. And they were all filled with the Holy Spirit, and began to SPEAK WITH OTHER TONGUES, as the Spirit gave them utterance."

As a result of this power from above that came down on them, people from different geographic regions (15 countries or areas) heard them speaking in their own languages about the mighty works of God. The people from the different nations and areas understood the tongues being spoken; however, the people doing the speaking (those filled with the Spirit) thought they were STRANGE LANGUAGES, or "other tongues": they did NOT understand them.

Some people hearing and seeing them were in doubt, saying "What does this mean?" Others were mocking and saying, "These men are full of new wine." But peter, full of the Holy Spirit, said, "These are not drunk with wine ... it is only 9:00 in the morning; but this is what the prophet Joel said would happen [800 years before]:

"It shall come to pass in the last days, says God, I will POUR OUT of my Spirit upon all flesh."

Peter, preaching to the crowd, explained to them what they were seeing and hearing. He told them Jesus had "poured out" the Holy Spirit on his followers.

"This Jesus has God raised up, whereof we are all witnesses. Therefore being by the right hand of God exalted, and having received of the Father the PROMISE of the Holy Spirit, he has shed forth (poured out) this, which you now see and hear." [Acts 2:32-33]

The baptism in the Holy Spirit is the "gift" of POWER which God promised!

The baptism in the Holy Spirit is NOT the same as baptism into the body of Christ (read 1 Corinthians 12:13). When a person is saved (at that very instant), the HOLY SPIRIT of God is the AGENT who places that person into the body of Christ: the brotherhood of all believers in Jesus.

In Acts 2:33 you can see that the baptism in the Holy Spirit happens when JESUS, as the AGENT, NOT the Holy Spirit, "pours out", or sheds forth, the Holy Spirit upon believers. This can happen at the time a person is saved or after they are saved. It can happen before water baptism or after.

The baptism in the Holy Spirit is the "gift" of POWER which God promised!

In Acts Chapter Ten (verses 44-46) we read of another case where the Holy Spirit was "poured out". The Apostle Peter was sent by God to preach the Gospel at the house of a man named Cornelius, a centurion in the Italian band of the Roman army.

"While Peter yet spoke these words, the Holy Spirit FELL on all them which heard the word. And they of the circumcision [the Jews] which believed were astonished, as many as came with Peter, because that on the Gentiles [non-Jews] also was POURED OUT the gift of the Holy Ghost. For they heard them SPEAK WITH TONGUES, and magnify [praise] God."

In Acts 19:1-6 we learn of an interesting case. The Apostle Paul came to the city of Ephesus and found some followers of John the Baptist. He said unto them, "Have you received the Holy Spirit since you believed?" They answered him, "We have not so much as heard whether there be any Holy Spirit."

These 12 men had been followers of John the Baptist and had been baptized by him, but they had never believed "on him who should come after him, that is, on Christ Jesus." Paul explained the way of salvation to them ... they believed on Christ Jesus and Paul baptized them in water. After this, "When Paul laid his hands upon them, the Holy

Spirit came upon them; and they SPOKE WITH TONGUES, and prophesied."

In Acts 2:4 (the first case we studied) when the followers of Jesus were filled with the Holy Spirit, they began to SPEAK WITH OTHER TONGUES. Now read the verses below (cases #2 and #3 we just studied), and notice what they have in common with Acts 2:4:

"For they heard them SPEAK WITH TONGUES, and magnify God." [Acts 10:46]

"And when Paul laid his hands upon them, the Holy Spirit came on them; and they SPOKE WITH TONGUES, and prophesied." [Acts 19:6]

In every case we have studied, we see that as a result of the power of God coming down upon them, they SPOKE IN TONGUES!

Remember the preacher, Paul, we just studied about? (Before he was saved, his name was Saul.) When he was saved, a bright light out of Heaven blinded him for three days. Just after he was saved, God sent a man named Ananias to pray for him. When Ananias laid hands on Saul, he prayed for two things:

That he might receive his sight; and,
That he might be filled with the Spirit.
[Acts 9:17-18]

Even though we don't read in the passage above about Paul speaking in tongues as a result of the Holy Spirit coming down upon him in power, we do know that Paul was a "tongues-speaker". In the book of First Corinthians, Paul said, "I thank my God, I SPEAK WITH TONGUES more than all of you." This was after Paul was filled with the Holy Spirit. [1 Corinthians 14:18]

Paul was not talking about a language he had studied such as Hebrew, Latin, Greek, or Aramaic, for then he would have understood what he was praying. When Paul prayed in tongues he did NOT understand it. We know this because in 1 Corinthians 14:14 he said, "If I pray in an unknown tongue, my spirit prays, but my understanding [my mind] is unfruitful."

What one thing seemed to happen each time the Holy Spirit came down upon people? THEY SPOKE IN TONGUES!

Have you ever been "baptized" in the Holy Spirit? If not, ask the Lord Jesus to baptize you right now. Pray and wait on God until you receive this POWER!

Tell the Lord how much you love him. Praise Him! While you are praising Him, simply shut off your own language or dialect and start praising Him in a NEW language the Holy Spirit will give you. You will not understand your new language, but don't let that bother you. "He that speaks in an unknown tongue speaks not unto men, but unto

12

God: for no man understands him; in the spirit he is speaking secret truths [to God]." [1 Corinthians 14:2]

Pray to God much in your new language. It will build you up. And then you will be able to build others up. 1 Corinthians 14:4 says, "He that speaks in an unknown tongue edifies [builds up] himself ..."

Now that you understand more about the Baptism in the Holy Spirit, let us review - and at the same time - study some extra benefits of this wonderful gift of God.

- ■ You become productive in God's kingdom;
- ■ You receive gifts of the Holy Spirit;
- ■ You pray in the language of the Spirit;
- ■ You become talented and creative!

PRODUCTIVE IN GOD'S KINGDOM

The baptism in the Holy Spirit enables you to produce more fruit. It gives you POWER! In John 15:17, Jesus said, "You have not chosen me, but I have chosen you, and ordained you, that you should go and bring forth FRUIT ..." Jesus was

NOT talking about the "fruit of the Spirit" which we read about in Galatians 5:22-23: Love, joy, peace, patience, kindness, goodness, humility, faithfulness, and self-control.

Jesus was talking about the fruit of a Christian. "You ... go and bring forth fruit." A lemon tree produces lemons; a banana tree produces bananas; a Christian produces Christians. The fruit of a Christian is "another Christian". Jesus said, "Herein is my Father glorified, that you bear much fruit; so shall you be my disciples." [John 15:7]

Sometimes you do not SEE power. Sometimes you do not HEAR power. Sometimes you do not FEEL power. But power is still power! Go in FAITH with the power you have asked for: the baptism in the Holy Spirit. Preach, witness for Christ, lay hands on the sick, cast out demons, distribute literature; you will then SEE, HEAR, and FEEL power ... miracles will happen!

GIFTS OF THE HOLY SPIRIT

The baptism in the Holy Spirit makes you a candidate to receive one or more of the "gifts" of the Holy Spirit. (Read about them in 1 Corinthians 12:4-11.)

The gifts of the Holy Spirit are as follows:

THE WISDOM GIFTS:

- The word of knowledge
- The word of wisdom
- Discerning of spirits

THE VOCAL GIFTS:

- Kinds of tongues
- Interpretation of tongues
- Prophecy

THE POWER GIFTS:

- Faith
- Gifts of healing
- The working of miracles

These gifts of the Spirit operate through you to enable you to:

1. Do God's work
2. Help other people
3. Live in victory
4. Build up the brotherhood of the believers

Now we will study how they operate.

THE WORD OF KNOWLEDGE

The word of knowledge is a word, or message, God gives you concerning a situation in a person's life, business, or ministry; not to discredit them or to embarrass them, but to help them know that God knows their situation. Sometimes the person may know about the situation already, but when the "word of knowledge" comes to them through you, it is a sign to them that God is aware of their situation ... and that he cares!

The person may not be aware of the situation, however, and God may be giving you a word of knowledge to reveal the situation to them. It may be an area of their Christian walk where they are under Satanic attack.

THE WORD OF WISDOM

Sometimes the word of knowledge and the word of wisdom are dual gifts. That is, sometimes they work together. Wisdom is knowledge in action; so a "word of wisdom" tells one WHAT to do in a given situation. For example, God may give you a word of KNOWLEDGE for someone who is having financial trouble, to tell them that demon forces are resisting finances from coming to them.

Then, God may give you a word of WISDOM for that same person to tell them what to do: to bind the demon forces in the name of Jesus, and "break their hold", commanding them "to depart and never come back", and then to have the person CALL IN (or, speak in) God's abundance! Sometimes the word of knowledge and the word of wisdom may come through different people.

● DISCERNING OF SPIRITS

Discerning of spirits is the ability to see or know:

1. The activity of the spirit world, both Holy Angels and demons.
2. What is of God from what is of the devil.

The gift of discernment is often used in conjunction with the gift of miracles and the gift of healing. You need to know every move of the Spirit of God and to discern it from the spirit of man and the spirit of the devil.

If you do not understand, God will explain it to you if you have this gift. Even though all people do not have the "gift" of discerning of spirits, still, God wants all his children to be discerning. As you get into God's Word, and God's Word gets into you - as you talk to and walk with God daily - you will begin to know when things and people are of God or not. You will discern.

KINDS OF TONGUES

Different kinds of tongues, or the ability to speak with strange languages, is different than praying in tongues, or praying in the Spirit. All who have been baptized in the Holy Spirit have the privilege and the ability to pray in tongues; however, not all have the "gift" of tongues. The gift of tongues is given to provide a message from God:

1. To a group of two or more believers (the Church);

2. To individuals who are Christians: or,

3. To unbelievers.

Once I was called to another city to pray for the wife of the General of the Armies of Chile, South America. Another person was interpreting for me in Spanish while I spoke English. After showing several Scriptures to the lady concerning how to know Christ, I led her in a prayer through the interpreter. I was filled with joy as she received Christ as her savior, and I started talking in tongues.

When she heard me speaking in tongues, the Chilean lady said to my interpreter, "He (Apostle Handley) is speaking ancient Aramaic." I told the interpreter, "Tell her I cannot speak that language; but God is giving her a sign to build her faith."

Earlier that day, in another city, I had been speaking in tongues in a home, and a visitor in that home said, "That man spoke in Aramaic." God gave two different people that day - in different cities - a "sign" through tongues to help them build their faith and believe the works of God!

● INTERPRETATION OF TONGUES

Interpretation of tongues is the ability from God to explain - or, interpret - the message in tongues. It is usually a dual gift used in conjunction with kinds of tongues. Sometimes the message in tongues and the interpretation in tongues may come through different people. When God's purpose for tongues is as a sign to unbelievers, there is NO need for interpretation because the unbelievers will understand the message in their language [1 Corinthians 14:22].

When God's purpose for tongues is as a message to the Church, it should be exercised by one or two people - at the most by three - and in turn, (or order, one after the other). One person should interpret [1 Corinthians 14:27-28]. If there is NO interpreter, let the person speaking in tongues be silent in the church, and let him speak to himself and to God. Let all things be done decently and in order.

● PROPHECY

Prophecy actually means to speak forth God's Word. Prophecy is not just teaching or preaching, although a teacher or a preacher may also be a prophet; prophecy is a "gift" given by God for edification, exhortation, and comfort. In other words, for help and encouragement.

The New Testament teaches that you are to " ... desire spiritual gifts, especially that you may prophesy." (1 Corinthians 14:1). The prophet Joel said 770 years before Christ, that "in the last days your sons and your daughters shall prophesy." (Joel 2:28.)

Be sure prophecy is based upon the Word of God. Isaiah 8:20 says, "To the law and to the testimony [the Bible]: If they speak not according to this word, it is because there is no light in them." Judge prophecy according to the Word of God.

The same practice should be true of tongues and interpretation: there should be no contradiction with the Holy Bible. Also, never seek direction from prophecy. If God has been speaking to you previously (in your heart) about a certain thing, then maybe all you need is a confirmation by one prophecy.

If you are not sure God is speaking to you about a matter, wait and God will reveal his will to you; first, in your spirit, and then possibly by confirming it "in the mouth of two or three witnesses" with prophecy. However, **get your direction from God ... not people!** Psalm 27:11 says, "Lead me in a plain path, O Lord, because of my enemies."

● FAITH

The Bible tells us that "God has dealt to every man the measure of faith." [Romans 12:3] However, the "gift" of faith is a special gift or ability (which God imparts to some people) to do exploits ... or to reach out in faith to do great works for God: for example, to evangelize every nation, tribe, tongue, and dialect of the earth for Christ.

● GIFTS OF HEALING

We read in 1 Corinthians 12:9, "The gifts of healing [given] by the same Spirit." The person who receives healing may be looked upon as receiving the gift. But in another sense, the person through whom God works as an instrument to heal the sick has received a definite "distribution" of God's Spirit called the "gift of healing".

Notice, the Bible says "gifts" of healing; not just one gift of healing. The Holy Spirit is God's agent on earth to supply the healing power of Christ. You must know God's compassion in healing.

God wants to make men whole in every area of their lives: spiritually, mentally, physically, materially, and socially. The gifts of healing operate to let people know that God cares for them and that he has made provision to help them here on earth as they walk with him, and as they serve him in love before they arrive in Heaven.

THE WORKING OF MIRACLES

Sometimes physical healings in the body are really the result of the working of creative miracles; such as eyeballs, ear drums, or voice boxes being created by God where there were none before, or where they had been destroyed. Healing may be slow or fast, but miracles (which produce healing) are usually instantaneous.

The working of miracles, however, is not just related to healing alone. Miracles are supernatural (extra-natural, "outside of nature") events to change the force of nature: as when Elisha caused the ax head to float, and when Elijah parted the Jordan River.

A few years ago the Lord directed me to go to the top of the Student Union at one of the largest universities in the USA and to preach from the roof with a loudspeaker. There was no way for my loudspeaker horn to be directed to the crowd below.

I knew God had sent me there to preach and that I needed a miracle. God blew the wind currents down in such a manner that the sound was on the ground where the people were. They were looking for me outside the building on the ground level ... but I was not there!

On another occasion, I was baptizing a man in the ocean at night near some very dangerous rocks. I prayed and asked God to help me as I did not know the waters. As soon as our feet touched the water, the ocean lighted up - like a giant light "under water" - so that we could even see the ocean bottom.   God kept the light on during the baptism and until we reached shore again; as soon as we took our feet out, the light went off.

The working of miracles may happen as a result of your faith, or simply because of the sovereignty of God: either way, it is a gift from God! Several engineers from Hughes Aircraft {General Motors] witnessed the ocean lighting up, some of whom later became top level management and one became an International Vice-President.

All of the gifts of the Spirit operate through the channel of faith. The INPUT to build your faith ... so that you will have a channel, or conductor, through which the gifts may operate ... is the Word of God. "So then faith comes by hearing, and hearing by the Word of God" [Romans 10:17].

The OUTPUT to release the gifts (via the channel of faith) is love. "Faith ... works by love" [Galatians 5:6]. So the Word of God builds your faith and gives you a channel through which the gifts can flow; then, love motivates you to allow the gifts to operate: whether you "feel" like it or not!

PRAY IN THE SPIRIT'S LANGUAGE

The Baptism in the Holy Spirit makes it possible for you to pray in the language of the Holy Spirit, in tongues. Not all who have received the baptism have the GIFT of tongues; but all who are baptized in the Holy Spirit have the ability AND the privilege to PRAY in tongues. There are several reasons why God gives you this language. Praying in tongues, in the Spirit, is a supernatural way to:

- Praise God;

- Build yourself up;

- Pray according to God's will.

PRAISE GOD

Remember what happened at the household of Cornelius, in Acts 10:44-46, when the Holy Spirit fell on them? "For they heard them speak with tongues, and magnify [praise] God." Have you ever wanted to praise God so much you just didn't have the words to express it?

You will not have this trouble when you praise God in the Spirit. Praise is very important because it builds an "atmosphere" for God to dwell in. The Bible says, "[God] inhabits the praises of Israel," in Psalm 22:3. When you praise God, you build a "bridge" for God to enter your situation and to help you.

● BUILD YOURSELF UP

Praying in the Spirit is a way of edifying yourself, or of building yourself up spiritually. In I Corinthians 14:4 we read, "He that speaks in a tongue edifies himself, but he that prophesies edifies the church." It is NOT selfish to want to build yourself up. You cannot build up others, including the Church, until you are built up!

● PRAY ACCORDING TO GOD'S WILL

The Holy Spirit knows what to pray for when you don't; the Spirit knows people and situations that you don't know about. Secondly, He knows the will of God, and how to pray for you concerning it. And thirdly, the Spirit of God prays around the limitations of your mind; that which your mind does NOT understand.

"For if I pray in an unknown tongue, my spirit prays, but my understanding [mind] is unfruitful" [I Corinthians 14:14]. "Likewise the Spirit also helps our infirmities [weaknesses]: for we know NOT what we should pray for as we ought ... and He [God] that searches the hearts knows what is the mind of the Spirit, because He [the Spirit] makes intercession for the saints according to the will of God." [Romans 8:26-27]

Once I was in a prayer meeting at the home of a friend, and a lady received a "word of knowledge" that somebody was about to commit suicide. A few minutes later, we heard sirens sounding; police cars and fire trucks were stopping across the boulevard, and a police helicopter was circling overhead while a large crowd was gathering.

I took my Bible with me and went to the crowd of people. When I came to the crowd, a woman was screeching [shrieking] like a wild animal as she rolled on the ground; she was demon-possessed. I laid my hands on the lady and started to pray in English, but as soon as I did, I realized, "I don't really know WHAT to pray for as I ought to."

The Lord Jesus impressed me to lay hands on the lady again and pray for her aloud in tongues. I waved my Bible to the crowd first, so they could know that what I was doing was about Jesus ...

and then laid my hands upon the lady, praying aloud for her in tongues. Immediately she became quiet and peaceful. I did not know WHAT to pray for her as I ought, but the Holy Spirit did. She was set free from the evil spirits.

TALENTED AND CREATIVE

The Baptism in the Holy Spirit may provide a person with a special spirit of ability or talent, such as:

> ➢ A spirit of craftsmanship;
> ➢ A spirit of music;
> ➢ A spirit of art;
> ➢ A spirit of creativity.

In Exodus 31, verses 1-11, a man named Bezaleel was filled with the spirit of God in wisdom, and in understanding, and in knowledge, and in all manner of workmanship. He was enabled by the Spirit to work in gold, silver, and brass; in cutting and setting stones, and in carving wood: to help in the building of the tabernacle.

Another example ... about 500 years later, King David said that the pattern of the temple which his son, Solomon, built was given to David "by the spirit". "All this," said David, "the Lord made me understand in writing by his hand upon me, even all the works of this pattern." [I Chronicles 28:12-19]

CONCLUSION

The "promise" of the Father, the "gift" which Jesus said He, himself, would send upon you, is a gift of power. With it, you have both the POWER and ABILITY to tell about Jesus and preach his "Good News" everywhere.

With this gift of power you can talk to God and praise him in the language of the Spirit. You can pray for the "unknown"... past the limitations of your mind. You can build yourself up ... and then, build others up. You can do NEW things: creative things ... things you could not do before. Also, the Spirit himself will distribute other new gifts to you - called the "gifts of the Spirit" - to help you in your personal life and in your service of love for God.

~ ~ ~

Prince Handley

Email prayer requests and praise reports to:
princehandley@gmail.com

Or write to:
Prince Handley
P.O. Box A
Downey, California 90241
USA